My First Voyage

Christopher Columbus

*Columbus's Letter to the Chancellor of the Exchequer, enclosing another
for their Highnesses, about the Islands found in the Indies*

Arms of Spain and Granada from *De Insulis inuentis*, Rome, 1493

With Pictures from the Incunabula of the Letter and Notes from Manuscript Variations

And pictures in the margins by Alan Archambault

Edited and Translated by R. H. Major

FIRST VOYAGE OF COLUMBUS.[1]

A Letter sent by Columbus to [Luis de Santangel] Chancellor of the Exchequer [of Aragon], respecting the Islands found in the Indies, enclosing another for their Highnesses.

SIR,—Believing that you will take pleasure in hearing of the great success which our Lord has granted me in my voyage, I write you this letter, whereby you will learn how in thirty-three days'[2] time I reached the Indies with the fleet which the most illustrious King and Queen, our Sovereigns, gave to me, where I found very many islands thickly peopled, of all which I took possession without resistance, for

---

Esta Carta embió Colon al Escrivano de Racion de las Islas halladas en las Indias. Contenida la otra de Sus Altezas.

Señor, por que se que aureis[3] plazer de la grand victoria que nuestro señor me ha dado en mi vyaie, vos escriuo esta por la qual sabreys commo en xxxiij dias pase a las jndias[4] con la armada que los illustrissimos Rey et reyna, nuestros señores, me dieron, donde yo falle muy muchas Islas pobladas con gente syn numero. Y dellas todas he tomado posession por sus altezas con pregon y

[1] The original spelling of the Ambrosian text, with all its faults, is here preserved, with the exception of the separation of words fused together, and the addition of punctuation and capitals for the sake of clearness. Suggested corrections from the other texts will be placed at the foot of each page, V. standing for Valencian text; S. for Simancas text; I. for Italian text; L. for Latin; D. for Dati. Such misspellings as a Spanish scholar will readily recognize as the blunders of the Spanish printer I have not thought it necessary to notice.

[2] From the 8th of September when Columbus sailed from the Canaries, to the 11th of October when he first saw land, was thirty-three days.

[3] Habreis.　　　　[4] V. " pasé de las Islas de Canaria a las Indias."

Fernãd⁹ rexhyſpanía

Fernando V, King of Spain

4

their Highnesses by proclamation made and with the royal standard unfurled. To the first island that I found I gave the name of *San Salvador*,[1] in remembrance of His High Majesty, who hath marvellously brought all these things to pass ; the Indians call it *Guanaham.* To the second island I gave the name of *Santa-Maria de Concepcion*,[2] the third I called *Fernandina*;[3] the fourth, *Isabella*;[4] the fifth, *Juana*;[5] and so to each one I gave a new name. When I reached *Juana,* I followed its coast to the westward, and found it so large that I thought it must be the mainland,—the province of *Cathay*; and, as I found neither towns nor villages on the sea-coast, but only a few hamlets, with the inhabitants, of which I could not hold conversation, because they all immediately fled, I kept on the same route, thinking that I could not fail to light upon some large cities and towns. At length, after the proceeding of many leagues, and finding that nothing new presented itself, and that the coast was leading

---

vandera real estendida, y non me fue contradicho. A la primera que yo falle puse nombre Sant Saluador, a comemoracion de Su Alta Magestad, el qual marauillosamente todo esto andado ;[6] los jndios la llaman Guanaham. A la segunda puse nombre la ylsa de santa Maria de Concepcion. A la tercera Ferrandina. A la quarta la Ysabella. A la quinta la isla Juana, et asy a cada vna nombre nueuo. Quando yo llegue a la Juana segui yo la costa della al poniente y la falle tan grande que pense que seria tierra firma, la prouincia de Cátayo, y como no falle asi[7] villas y lugares en la costa de la mar, salvo pequeñas poblaciones, conla gente de las quales non podia hauer fabla, por que luego fuyan todos, andaua yo adelante por el dicho camino, pensando de no errar grandes Ciudades o villas, y al cabo de muchas leguas visto que no hauia innovacion y que la costa me leuaua al setentrion, de adonde mi voluntad era contraria, por que el yuierno era ya encarnado, yo

---

[1] *San Salvador* now.   [2] Long Island.   [3] Great Exuma.
[4] Saometo or Crooked Island.   [5] Cuba.
[6] V. and S. " ha dado."   [7] V. " ahi."

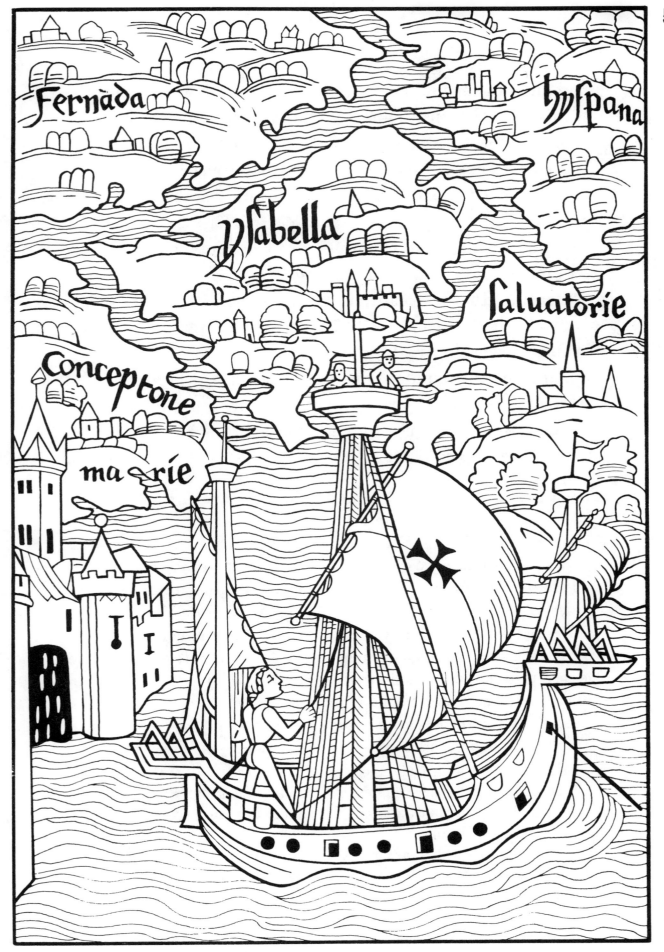

Christopher Columbus on the *Santa Maria*

me northwards (which I wished to avoid, because winter had already set in, and it was my intention to move southwards; and because moreover the winds were contrary), I resolved not to wait for a change in the weather, but returned to a certain harbour which I had remarked, and from which I sent two men ashore to ascertain whether there was any king or large cities in that part. They journeyed for three days and found countless small hamlets with numberless inhabitants, but with nothing like order; they therefore returned. In the meantime I had learned from some other Indians whom I had seized, that this land was certainly an island; accordingly, I followed the coast eastward for a distance of one hundred and seven leagues, where it ended in a cape. From this cape, I saw another island to the eastward at a distance of eighteen leagues from the former, to which I gave the name of *La Española*.[1] Thither I went,

---

tenia proposito de hazer del[2] al austro y tanbien el viento me dio adelante, determine de no aguardar otro tiempo, y bolui atras fasta un señalado puerto da donde enbie dos hombres por la tierra para saber si auia rey o grandes ciudades. Andouieron tres iornadas y hallaron infinitas poblaciones pequeñas y gente sin numero, mas no cosa de regimiento, por lo qual se boluieron. Yo entendia harta de otros jndios que ya tenia tomados commo continuamente esta tierra era isla, et asi segui la costa della al oriente ciento y siete leguas faste donde fazia fin : del qual cabo vi[3] otra isla al oriente, distincta[4] de esta diez o ocho leguas, a la qual luego puse nombre la Spañola, y fui alli y segui la parte del setentrion asi commo de la Juana al oriente, clxxviij[5] grandes leguas[6] por linia recta del

[1] Hispaniola or San Domingo.

[2] So in all the texts. Senhor de Varnhagen suggests " hacerme."

[3] V. and S. " habia otra isla ;" L. " aliam insulam prospexi."

[4] V. and S. " distante."

[5] V. " ciento e ochenta y ocho." S. " ciento e setenta y ocho." I. " cento otanta otto leghe." L. " miliaria dlxiiii." D. " cinquecensessantaquattro miglia."

[6] V. " leguas la cual y todas.

From the rhymed Italian edition of Giuliano Dati, *La Lettera Dellisole Che Ha Trovato Nuovamente Il Re Dispagna*, Florence, 1493

Christopher Columbus meets the Taino on Hispaniola. King Ferdinand is on his throne across the sea.

and followed its northern coast to the eastward (just as I had done with the coast of *Juana*), one hundred and seventy[1]-eight full leagues due east. This island, like all the others, is extraordinarily large, and this one extremely so. In it are many seaports with which none that I know in Christendom can bear comparison, so good and capacious that it is wonder to see. The lands are high, and there are many very lofty mountains with which the island of *Cetefrey* cannot be compared. They are all most beautiful, of a thousand different shapes, accessible, and covered with trees of a thousand kinds of such great height that they seemed to reach the skies. I am told that the trees never lose their foliage, and I can well understand it, for I observed that they were as green and luxuriant as in Spain in the month of May. Some were in bloom, others bearing fruit, and others otherwise according to their nature. The nightingale was singing as well as other birds of a thousand different kinds; and that, in November, the month in which I myself was roaming amongst them. There are palm-trees of six or eight

---

oriente asi commo de la Juana, la qual y todas las otras son fortissimas[2] en demasiado grado, y esta en estremo ; en ella ay muchos puertos enla costa dela mar, sin comparacion de otros que yo sepa en christianos, y sartos, y buenos, y grandes, que es marauilla. Las tierras della son altas y en ella muy muchas sierras y montañas altissimas sin comparacion de ysla de centre.[3] Son todas fermossimas de mill. fechuras y todas andabiles y llenas de arboles de mil maneras y altas y pareçen que llegan al cielo ; y tengo por dicho que jamas pierden la foia, segun lo puede comprehender que los vi tan verdes y tan hermosos commo son por Mayo en Spaña, y dellos stavan floridos, dellos con fruto, y dellos en otro termino segun es su calidad ; y cantaua el ruiseñol y otros paxaricos de mil maneras en el mes de nouienbre por alli donde yo andaua. Ay

[1] It should be 188 leagues.
[2] V. "fertilisimas." S. "fortisimas." I. "feralissime."
[3] V. "Teneryfe." S. "Cetrefrey." I. "Santaffer." L. omitted.

kinds, wonderful in their beautiful variety ; but this is the case with all the other trees and fruits and grasses ; trees, plants, or fruits filled us with admiration. It contains extraordinary pine groves, and very extensive plains. There is also honey, a great variety of birds, and many different kind of fruits. In the interior there are many mines of metals and a population innumerable. *Española* is a wonder. Its mountains and plains, and meadows, and fields, are so beautiful and rich for planting and sowing, and rearing cattle of all kinds, and for building towns and villages. The harbours on the coast, and the number and size and wholesomeness of the rivers, most of them bearing gold, surpass anything that would be believed by one who had not seen them. There is a great difference between the trees, fruits, and plants of this island and those of *Juana*. In this island there are many spices and extensive mines of gold and other metals. The inhabitants of this and of all the other islands I have found or gained intelligence of, both men and women, go as naked as they were born, with the

---

palmas de seys[1] o de ocho maneras, que es admiracion verlas por la disformidad fermosa dellas; mas asi commo los otros arboles y frutos et yeruas. En ella ay pinares a marauilla, e ay canpiñas grandissimas et ay mjel, y de muchas maneras, de aues y frutas muy diversas. En las tierras ay muchas minas de metales et ay gente inestimable numero. La spañola es marauilla; las sierras y las montañas y las uegas y las campiñas y las tierras tan fermosas y gruesas para plantar et senbrar, para criar ganados de todas suertes para hedificios de villas y lugares. Los puertos de la mar aqui no hauria creancia sin vista, et delos rios muchos y grandes y buenas aguas, los mas delos quales traen oro. En los arboles et frutos et yeruas ay grandes diferencias de aquellas de la Juana. En esta ay muchas specierias[2] y grandes minas de oro y d'otros metales. La gente desta jsla et de todas las otras que he fallado y hauido,[3] in aya hauido noticia, andan todos desnudos, hombres et mugeres, asi

---

[1] V. and S. "seis." I. "setto." L. "septem." D. "septe."
[2] V. and S. "especies." [3] V. and S. "y ha havido.

exception that some of the women cover one part only with a single leaf of grass or with a piece of cotton, made for that purpose. They have neither iron, nor steel, nor arms, nor are they competent to use them, not that they are not well-formed and of handsome stature, but because they are timid to a surprising degree. Their only arms are reeds cut in the seeding time,[1] to which they fasten small sharpened sticks, and even these they dare not use; for on several occasions it has happened that I have sent ashore two or three men to some village to hold a parley, and the people have come out in countless numbers, but, as soon as they saw our men approach, would flee with such precipitation that a father would not even stop to protect his son; and this not because any harm had been done to any of them, for, from the first, wherever I went and got speech with them, I gave them of all that I had, such as cloth and many other things, without receiving anything in return,

---

commo sus madres los paren, avnque algunas mugeres se cobijan vn solo lugar con vna sola foia de yerua o vna cosa[2] de algodon que para ellos fazen. Ellos no tienen fierro ni azero ni armas, ni son para ello; no porque no sea gente bien dispuesta et de fermosa estatura, saluo que son muy temerosos a marauilla. No tienen otras armas saluo las armas de las cañas, quando estan con la simiente, a la qual ponen al cabo vn palillo agudo, et no osan usar de aquellas, que muchas vezes me ha acaescido enbiar a tierra dos o tres honbres alguna villa para hauer fabla, y salir a ellos dellos sin numero, et despues que los veyan llegar, fuyan a no aguárdar padre a hijo, y esto no porque a ninguno se aya fecho mal; antes a toda cabo a donde yo ay estado et podido auer fabla, les he dado de todo lo que tenia, asi paño commo otras cosas muchas, sin recebir por ello cosa alguna; mas son asi temerosos sin remedio. Verdad es que despues que aseguran y pierden esta miedo, ellos son tanto sin engaño y tan liberales delo que tienen que no lo

[1] These canes are probably the flowering stems of large grasses, similar to the bamboo or to the arundinaria used by the natives of Guiana for blowing arrows. [2] V. "cofia." S. "cosa." I. "cosa."

but they are, as I have described, incurably timid. It is
true that when they are reassured and have thrown off this
fear, they are guileless, and so liberal of all they have that
no one would believe it who had not seen it. They never
refuse anything that they possess when it is asked of them;
on the contrary, they offer it themselves, and they exhibit so
much loving kindness that they would even give their hearts;
and, whether it be something of value or of little worth that
is offered to them, they are satisfied. I forbade that worth-
less things, such as pieces of broken porringers and broken
glass, and ends of straps, should be given to them; although,
when they succeeded in obtaining them, they thought they
possessed the finest jewel in the world. It was ascertained
that a sailor received for a leather strap a piece of gold
weighing two *castellanos*[1] and a half, and others received for
other objects of far less value, much more. For new *blancas*[2]
they would give all that they had, whether it was two or three
castellanos in gold or one or two arrobas[3] of spun cotton.
They took even bits of the broken hoops of the wine barrels,

---

creerian sino el que lo viese. Ellos de cosa que tengan pidiendo
gela, iamas dizen de no; antes conuidan la persona con ello, y
muestran tanto amor que darian los coraçones, et quieren sea cosa
de valor quien sea de poco precio luego por qualquiera cosica de
qualquiera manera que sea que sele de por ello, sean contentos.
Yo defendi que no se les diesen cosas tan siuiles commo pedaços
de escudillas rotas, y pedaços de vidrio roto, y cabos de agugetas:
aunque quando ellos esto podran llegar,[4] los parescia auer
la mejor joya del mundo: que se açerto auer vn marinero por
vna agugeta de oro de peso de dos castellanos y medio, y otros
de otras cosas que muy menos valian, mucho mas. Ya por blancas
nueuas dauan por ellas todo quanto tenian auer que fuesen dos
ni tres castellanos de oro o vna arroua o dos de algodon fylado,

[1] An old Spanish coin.
[2] Small copper coins.
[3] One *arroba* weighs twenty-five pounds. [4] V. "llevar.

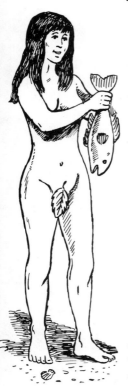

and gave, like fools, all that they possessed in exchange, insomuch that I thought it was wrong, and forbade it. I gave away a thousand good and pretty articles which I had brought with me in order to win their affection; and that they might be led to become Christians, and be well inclined to love and serve their Highnesses and the whole Spanish nation, and that they might aid us by giving us things of which we stand in need, but which they possess in abundance. They are not acquainted with any kind of worship, and are not idolaters; but believe that all power and, indeed, all good things are in heaven; and they are firmly convinced that I, with my vessels and crews, came from heaven, and with this belief received me at every place at which I touched, after they had overcome their apprehension. And this does not spring from ignorance, for they are very intelligent, and navigate all these seas, and relate everything to us, so that it is astonishing what a good account they are able to give of everything; but they have never seen men with clothes on, nor vessels like ours. On my reaching the Indies,

---

Fasta los pedaços delos arcos rotos de las pipas tomauan y dauan lo que tenian commo bestias, asy que me parescia mal. Yo lo defendi y daua yo graciosas mil cosas buenas que yo leuaua, por que tomen amor y allenda desto se faran[1] cristianos, que se jnclinan al amor y servicio de sus altezas y de toda la nacion castellana, y procuran de aiuntar[2] de nos dar de las cosas que tienen en abundancia que nos son neçessarias. Y no conocian ninguna seta nin ydolatria, saluo que todos creen que las fuerças y el bien es en el cielo. Y creyan muy firme que yo con estos nauios y gente venia del cielo, y en tal catamiento me recibian[3] en todo cabo despues de auer perdido el miedo. Y esto no precede porque sean ygnorantes, saluo de muy sotil ingenio y hombres que nauegan todas aquellas mares, que es marauilla la buena cuenta quellos dan de todo, salvo porque nunca vieron gente vestida ny semejantes nauios. Y luego que legue a las jndias en la primera ysla que halle, tome por fuerça algunos dellos para que depren-

[1] V. " façan."   [2] V. and S. " ayudar."   [3] V. and S. " reciben."

A Caravel, similar to Columbus's *Santa Maria*

I took by force, in the first island that I discovered, some of
these natives, that they might learn our language and give me
information in regard to what existed in these parts ; and it
so happened that they soon understood us and we them, either
by words or signs, and they have been very serviceable to us.
They are still with me, and, from repeated conversations that
I have had with them, I find that they still believe that I come
from heaven. And they were the first to say this wherever
I went, and the others ran from house to house and to the
neighbouring villages, crying with a loud voice : "Come,
come, and see the people from heaven !" And thus they all,
men as well as women, after their minds were at rest about
us, came, both large and small, and brought us something
to eat and drink, which they gave us with extraordinary
kindness. They have in all these islands very many canoes
like our row-boats : some larger, some smaller, but most of
them larger than a barge of eighteen seats. They are not so
wide, because they are made of one single piece of timber,
but a barge could not keep up with them in rowing, because
they go with incredible speed, and with these canoes they

---

diesen y me diesen notia delo que auia en aquellas partes, et asy
fue que luego entendiron, y nos a ellos, quando por lengua o señas,
y estos han aprouechado mucho. Oy en dia los traygo que siempre
estan de proposito que vengo del cielo por mucha conuersacion
que ayan auido conmigo, y estos eran los primeros a pronunciarlo
adonde yo llegaua ; y los otros andauan corriendo de casa en
casa, y alas villas çercenas con bozes altas, venid, venid a ver la
gente del cielo. Asi todos, hombres commo mugeres, despues de
auer el coraçon seguro de nos, venian que no quedauan grande ni
pequeño, y todos trayan algo de comer y de beuer que dauan con
un amor marauilloso. Ellos tienen todas las yslas muy muchas
canoas a manera de fustes de remo, dellas maioras, dellas menores
y algunas y muchas son mayoras que vna fusta de diez et ocho
bancos. No son tan anchas porque son de vn solo madero, mas
vna fusta no terna con ellas al remo porque van que no es cosa
de crer, y con estas nauegan todas aquellas yslas que son

navigate among these islands, which are innumerable, and carry on their traffic. I have seen in some of these canoes seventy and eighty men, each with his oar. In all these islands I did not notice much difference in the appearance of the inhabitants, nor in their manners nor language, except that they all understand each other, which is very singular, and leads me to hope that their Highnesses will take means for their conversion to our holy faith, towards which they are very well disposed. I have already said how I had gone one hundred and seven leagues in following the sea-coast of *Juana* in a straight line from west to east : and from that survey I can state that the island is larger than England and Scotland together, because, beyond these one hundred and seven leagues, there lie to the west two provinces which I have not yet visited, one of which is called *Avan*, where the people are born with a tail. These two provinces cannot be less in length than from fifty to sixty leagues, from what can be learned from the Indians that I have with me, and who are acquainted with all these islands. The other,

---

jnnumerables, y traten sus mercaderias. Algunas destas canoas he visto con. lxx. y lxxx. honbres en ella, y cada vno con su remo. En todas estas yslas no vide mucha diuersidad de la fechura dela gente ni en las costumbres ni en la lengua, saluo que todos se entienden, que es cosa muy singular, para lo que espero que determinaren sus altezas para la conversacion[1] dellos de nuestra santa fe a la qual son muy dispuestos. Ya dixe commo yo hauia andada c.vij. leguas por la costa de la mar por la derecha liña de ocidente a oriente por la ysla Juana, segun el qual camino puedo desir que esta isla es mayor que inglaterra y escosia juntas por que allen de destas c.vij. leguas, me queda de la parte de poniente dos prouincias que yo no he andado; la vna de las quales llaman Auan,[2] adonde nascen la gente con cola, las quales prouincias no pueden tener en longura menos de l. o lx. leguas, segund puede[3] entender destos jndios que yo tengo, los quales saben todas las

---

[1] V. and S. " conversion." L. " conversionem."
[2] V. " Nhan." S. " Cibau." L. " Anan." [3] V. and S. " puedo."

Española, has a greater circumference than all Spain, from Catalonia by the sea-coast to Fuenterabia in Biscay, since on one of its four sides I made one hundred and eighty-eight great leagues in a straight line from west to east. This is something to covet, and when found not to be lost sight of. Although I have taken possession of all these islands in the name of their Highnesses, and they are all more abundant in wealth than I am able to express; and although I hold them all for their Highnesses, so that they can dispose of them quite as absolutely as they can of the kingdoms of Castile, yet there was one large town in *Española* of which especially I took possession, situated in a locality well adapted for the working of the gold mines, and for all kinds of commerce, either with the main land on this side, or with that beyond which is the land of the great Khan, with which there will be vast commerce and great profit. To that city I gave the name of *Villa de Navidad*, and fortified it with a

---

yslas. Esta otra española en cierco tiene mas que la españa toda desde colunya[1] por costa de mar fasta fuente rauia en vi scaya pues en vna quadra anduue clxxxviij.[2] grandes leguas por recta linia de occidente a oriente. Esta es para desear, et vista, es para nunca dexar; enla qual puesto que de todas tenga tomada possession por sus altezas, y todas sean mas abastadas delo que yo se y puedo dezir, y todas las tengo por de sus altezas qual dellas pueden disponer commo y tan complidamente commo delos Reynos de castilla. En esta española en el lugar[3] mas conuenible y meyor comarca para las minas del oro y de todo trato, asi dela tierra firme de aqua commo de aquella de alla del grand can, adonde aura[4] grand trato et grand gançana, he tomado possession de vna villa grande, ala qual puse nombre la villa de Nauidad. Y en ella he fecho fuerça y fortaleza que ya a estas horas estara del

[1] V. "Colibre." S. "Colunia." L. "Colonia." Misread from an abridged word in the original, which the sense of the passage would make "Catalonia."

[2] V. and S. "ciento treinta y ocho." L. "miliaria dxl." D. "cinquecensessantoquattro miglia."[3] V. and S. "en lugar."[4] V. and S. "habra."

Insula hyspana

Christopher Columbus lands on Hispaniola. He did not have a Mediterranean galley, as we all know.

fortress, which by this time will be quite completed, and I have left in it a sufficient number of men with arms,[1] artillery, and provisions for more than a year, a barge, and a sailing master skilful in the arts necessary for building others. I have also established the greatest friendship with the king of that country, so much so that he took pride in calling me his brother, and treating me as such. Even should these people change their intentions towards us and become hostile, they do not know what arms are, but, as I have said, go naked, and are the most timid people in the world; so that the men I have left could, alone, destroy the whole country, and this island has no danger for them, if they only know how to conduct themselves. In all those islands it

---

todo acabada, y he dexada en ella gente que abasta para semejante fecho, con armas y artellarias et vituallas por mas de un año; y fusta y maestro de la mar en todas artes para fazer otras, y grande amistad con el rey de aquella tierra en tanto grado que se preciaua de me llamar y tener por hermano; y aunque le mudasse la voluntad a offender esta gente, el ni los suyos no saben que sean armas y andan desnudos commo ya he dicho: son los mas temerosos que ay en el mundo, asi que solamente la gente que alla queda, es para destroir toda aquella tierra, y es ysla syn peligro de sus personas sabiendo se regir. En todas estas yslas me parece que todos los honbres sean contentos con vna muger, y a su mayoral

[1] There appears to be a doubt as to the exact number of men left by Columbus at Española, different accounts variously giving it as thirty-seven, thirty-eight, thirty-nine, and forty. There is, however, a list of their names included in one of the diplomatic documents printed in Navarrete's work, which makes the number amount to forty, independent of the governor Diego de Arana, and his two lieutenants Pedro Gutierrez and Rodrigo de Escobedo. All these men were Spaniards, with the exception of two; one an Irishman named William Ires, a native of Galway, and one an Englishman, whose name was given as Tallarte de Lajes, but whose native designation it is difficult to guess at. The document in question, was a proclamation to the effect that the heirs of those men should, on presenting at the office of public business at Seville, sufficient proof of their being the next of kin, receive payment in conformity with the royal order to that purpose, issued at Burgos, 20 December, 1507.

seems to me that the men are content with one wife, except their chief or king, to whom they give twenty. The women seem to me to work more than the men. I have not been able to learn whether they have any property of their own. It seemed to me that what one possessed belonged to all, especially in the matter of eatables. I have not found in those islands any monsters, as many imagined; but, on the contrary, the whole race is very well-formed, nor are they black, as in Guinea, but their hair is flowing, for they do not dwell in that part where the force of the sun's rays is too powerful. It is true that the sun has very great power there, for the country is distant only twenty-six degrees from the equinoctial line. In the islands where there are high mountains, the cold this winter was very great, but they endure it, not only from being habituated to it, but by eating meat with a variety of excessively hot spices. As to savages, I did not even hear of any, except at an island which lies the

---

o rey dan fasta veynte. Las mugeres me parece que trabaian mas que los honbres, ni he podido entender si tenien bienes propios, que me parecio ver que aquello que vno tenia todos hazian parte, en especial de las cosas comederas. En estas yslas fasta aqui no he hallado honbres mostrudos, commo muchos pensauan; mas antes es toda gente de muy lindo acatamiento, ny son negros commo en guinea, saluo con sus cabellos corredios,[1] y no se crian adonde ay jnpeto[2] demasiado delos rayos solares. Es verdad quel sol tiene alli grande fuerça, puesto que es didistinta[3] dela linia inquinocial xxvi. grandes. En estas islas adonde ay montañas, ay tenida[4] a fuerça el frio este yuierno, mas ellos lo sufren por la costumbre que con la ayuda delas viandas que comen con[5] especias muchas y muy calientes en demasia. Asy que mostruos no he hallado jnnoticia, saluo de una ysla que es aqui en la segunda a la entrada

[1] V. and S. " correndios."
[2] V. " effeto." S. " espeto." Navarrete says that in old Spanish " espeto " meant a " spit." [3] V. and S. " distante."
[4] V. and S. " ahi tenia fuerza."
[5] V. and S. " como son." L. " quibus vescuntur."

second in one's way in coming to the Indies.[1] It is inhabited by a race which is regarded throughout these islands as extremely ferocious, and eaters of human flesh. These possess many canoes, in which they visit all the Indian islands, and rob and plunder whatever they can. They are no worse formed than the rest, except that they are in the habit of wearing their hair long, like women, and use bows and arrows made of reeds, with a small stick at the end, for want of iron, which they do not possess. They are ferocious amongst these exceedingly timid people; but I think no more of them than of the rest. These are they which have intercourse with the women of Matenino,[2] the first island one comes to on the way from Spain to the Indies, and in which there are no men. These women employ themselves in no labour suitable to their sex; but use bows and arrows made of reeds like those above described, and arm and cover themselves with plates of copper, of which metal they have a

From the portrait of Columbus by Tobias Stimmer

de las jndias, que es poblada de vna gente que tienen en todas las yslas por muy ferozes, los quales comen carne humana.[3] Estos tienen muchas canaos, con las quales corren todas las yslas de jndia: roban y toman quanto pueden. Ellos no son mas difformes que los otros, saluo que tienen en costumbre de traer los cabellos largos commo mugeres, y vsan arcos y flechas de las mismas armas de cañas con vn palillo al cabo, por defecto de fierro, que no tienen. Son feroses entre estos otros pueblos que son en demasiado grado couardes, mas yo no lo tengo a nada mas que a los otros. Estos son aquellos que tratan con las mugeres de matremonio,[4] que es la primera ysla partiendo despaña para las jndias que se falla, enla qual no ay honbre ninguno. Ellas no vsan exercicio femenil, saluo arcos y flechas commo los sobredichos de cañas, y se arman y cobijan con lamines de arambre, de que tienen mucho. Otra ysla me seguran mayor que la española, en que las

[1] Dominica. [2] Martinique.

[3] V. and S. " viva." L. " humana."

[4] V. " que tomaban las mugeres de Matinino." S. " que trocaban las mugeres de matrimonio." L. " qui coeunt cum quibusdam feminis quæ insulam Mateunim habitant." D. " isola decta Matanino."

great quantity. They assure me that there is another island larger than *Española*, in which the inhabitants have no hair. It is extremely rich in gold; and I bring with me Indians taken from these different islands, who will testify to all these things. Finally, and speaking only of what has taken place in this voyage, which has been so hasty, their Highnesses may see that I shall give them all the gold they require, if they will give me but a very little assistance; spices also, and cotton, as much as their Highnesses shall command to be shipped; and mastic, hitherto found only in Greece, in the island of Chios, and which the Signoria[1] sells at its own price, as much as their Highnesses shall command to be shipped; lign aloes, as much as their Highnesses shall command to be shipped; slaves, as many of these idolators as their Highnesses shall command to be shipped. I think also I have found rhubarb and cinnamon, and I shall find a thousand other valuable things by means of the men that I have left behind me, for I tarried at no point so long

personas no tienen ningun cabello. En esta ay oro sin cuenta, y desta y de las otras traigo comigo jndios para testimonio. Y conclusion a fablar desto solamente que sea fecho este viage, que fue si de corrida que pueden ver sus altezas que yo les dare oro quanto ovieren[2] menester con muy poquita ajuda que sus altezas me daran, agora specieria y algodon quanto sus altezas mandaran cargar, y almastica[3] quanta mandaran cargar, et dela qual fasta oy no se ha fallado, saluo en grecia enla ysla de xio, y el señorio la vende commo quiere, y liguñaloe quanto mandaran cargar, y esclavos quanto mandaran cargar et seran delos ydolatres.[4] Y creo auer hallado ruybaruo y canela y otras mil cosas de sustancia fallare, que auran fallado la gente que yo alla dexo, por que yo no me he detenido ningun cabo, en quanto el viento me aya dado lugar de

[1] Of Genoa. The island of Chios belonged to the Genoese Republic from 1346 to 1566.

[2] V. and S. "hobieren."   [3] V. and S. "almasiga."

[4] In the corrupt edition of the Latin translation reprinted by Navarrete from the *España Illustrada*, this word is rendered "hydrophilatorum."

as the wind allowed me to proceed, except in the town of *Navidad*, where I took the necessary precautions for the security and settlement of the men I left there. Much more I would have done if my vessels had been in as good a condition as by rights they ought to have been. This is much, and praised be the eternal God, our Lord, who gives to all those who walk in his ways victory over things which seem impossible; of which this is signally one, for, although others may have spoken or written concerning these countries, it was all mere conjecture, as no one could say that he had seen them—it amounting only to this, that those who heard listened the more, and regarded the matter rather as a fable than anything else. But our Redeemer hath granted this victory to our illustrious King and Queen and their kingdoms, which have acquired great fame by an event of such high importance, in which all Christendom ought to rejoice, and which it ought to celebrate with great festivals and the offering of solemn thanks to the Holy Trinity with many solemn prayers, both for the great exaltation which

nauegar, solamente enla villa de Nauidad en quanto dexe asegurado et bien asentado; y ala verdad mucho mas ficiera si los nauios me siruieran commo razon demandaua. Esto es harto[1] y eterno dios nuestro señor el qual da a todos aquellos que andan su camino victoria de cosas que parecen inposibles : y esta señaladamente fue la vna; porque avnque destas tierras ayan fallado o escripto,[2] todo va por conlectura sin allegar devista, saluo comprendiendo a tanto que los oyentes los mas escuchauan y juzgauan mas por fabla que por poca[3] cosa dello.

Asy que pues nuestro redentor dio victoria a nuestros illustrissimos rey et reyna y a sus reynos famosos de tan alta cosa, adonde toda la christianidad deve tomar alegria y fazer grandes fiestas, y dar gracias solennes a la santa trinidad con muchas oraciones solennes por el tanto enxalçamiento que auran, en

[1] V. and S. " cierto."
[2] V. and S. " fablado otros." L. " scripserunt vel locuti sunt."
[3] V. and S. " otra." L. " prope videbatur fabula."

may accrue to them in turning so many nations to our holy faith, and also for the temporal benefits which will bring great refreshment and gain, not only to Spain, but to all Christians. This, thus briefly, in accordance with the events.

Done on board the caravel, off the Canary Islands, on the fifteenth of February, fourteen hundred and ninety-three.

At your orders. THE ADMIRAL.

After this letter was written, as I was in the sea of Castille, there arose a south-west wind, which compelled me to lighten my vessels and run this day into this port of Lisbon, an event which I consider the most marvellous thing in the world, and whence I resolved to write to their High-

---

tornandose[1] tantos pueblosa nuestra santa fe, y despues por los bienes temporales ; que no solamente a la españa mas a todos los cristianos ternan aqui refrigerio y ganancia. Esto segun el fecho asi en breue[2]. Fecha enla calauera[3] sobre las yslas de cana-ria[4] a xv.[5] de febrero, Mill. y quatrocientos y nouenta y tres años.

Fara[6] lo que mandereys[7].

EL ALMIRANTE.

Nyma[8] que venia dentro en la carta.

Despues desta escripto :[9] y estando en mar de Castilla salyo tanto viento conmigo sul y sueste que me ha fecho descargar los nauios por cori[10] aqui en esto puerto de lysbona oy, que fue la mayor marauilla del mundo. Adonde acorde escriuir a sus altezas.

[1] V. and S. " ayuntandose."

[2] V. and S. " esto segundo ha fecho ser muy breve." L. " hæc ut gesta sunt sic breviter enarrata." [3] V. and S. " carabela." ·

[4] V. " la isla de Sa. Maria."

[5] V. " 18." This latter date is the only one which corresponds with the fourteen days, mentioned in the postscript, during which Columbus was detained at sea by the weather previously to his reaching Lisbon on the 4th of March.

[6] V. " Para." [7] V. " mandaredes."

[8] S. " Anima." V. The entire nema wanting. The same in L. and D. [9] S. " escrita." [10] S. " correr."

nesses. In all the Indies I have always found the weather like that in the month of May. I reached them in thirty-three days, and returned in twenty-eight, with the exception that these storms detained me fourteen days knocking about in this sea. All seamen say that they have never seen such a severe winter nor so many vessels lost.

Done on the fourteenth day of March.

En todas las yndias he siempre hallado los tenporales[1] commo en mayo. Adonde yo fuy en xxxiij.[2] dias y bolui en xxviij.[3] salvo questas tormentas me han detenido xiiij.[4] dias corriendo por esta mar. Dizen aqua todos los honbres dela mar que jamas ouo tan mal yuierno, no ni tantas perdidas de naues.[5] Fecha a. xiiij dias de marco.

Esta carta embio Colon al escrivano Deracion delas Islas halladas en las Indias. Contenida a otra[6] de sus Altezas.

[1] S. "tiempos." [2] S. "noventa y tres."
[3] S. "setenta y ocho." Both are wrong. It should be **forty-eight**, from January 16 to March 4. [4] S. "trece."
[5] S. "los quatro." Columbus really arrived at Lisbon on the 4th of March.
[6] S. "Indias e otra."